A CONTINENT OF
CREATURES

The Animals of
AUSTRALIA

Nicole K. Orr

PURPLE TOAD
PUBLISHING

Much of Australia is made up of desert. This means almost all Australians live on the coast where it is cooler.

Welcome to Australia (os-TRAY-lee-ah), the largest island in the world! The seasons here are opposite of those in North America. When it is summer in North America, it is winter in Australia.

The winters here can be almost as hot as the summers. Snow can only be found on the island of Tasmania. Australia's biomes range from the Outback's desert to the rain forest on the coast. In the north lies the grassy savanna.

The red kangaroo lives in the red desert of the Outback. With its strong legs and large feet, it can hop along at 35 miles per hour. Mother kangaroos have a pouch for carrying joeys (baby kangaroos).

Joeys grow strong by playing games.

The sugar glider is active at night. It spreads its limbs to glide through the treetops. Thin webs of skin between its toes and its fingers are what keep the animal overhead.

Sugar gliders can leap the length of a football field.

Koalas (koh-AH-laz) live in the eucalyptus (yoo-kuh-LIP-tus) trees of eastern and southeastern Australia. These marsupials (mar-SOO-pee-alz) sometimes sleep for 20 hours a day.

The Tasmanian **(taz-MAY-nee-an)** devil lives on the island of Tasmania. When this marsupial gets angry, it will bare its teeth, growl, and lunge. Baby Tasmanian devils are called imps.

The platypus (PLAT-ah-pus) lives near rivers and streams. Its snout looks like a duck's bill, and its tail is like a beaver's. A platypus holds its breath while it dives underwater to find worms, insects, and freshwater shrimp. The male has sharp spurs on its hind legs that hold venom to use for protection.

A platypus does not have a stomach.

The ibis doesn't have feathers on its head.

Some magpies swoop at people during nesting season.

Australia's cities are full of birds. The ibis (IY-bis) has a curved beak and three-toed feet that look like a dinosaur's. Bike riders and mail carriers have to watch out for the magpie. Why? To protect their chicks, the male magpie will dive at humans who come too close to the nest.

A kookaburra's beak can be four inches long.

Cassowary (Cas-oh-wayr-ee) have three toes on each foot with sharp claws.

The cassowary cannot fly, but it sure can run — up to 30 miles per hour! It is almost as tall as a human and will run right at a person to attack.

The laughing kookaburras (KOOK-ah-bur-ahz) will wake the rain forest at sunrise with their loud laughter. Kookaburras eat mostly snakes and reptiles, but they also like earthworms and mice.

The green sea turtle and mandarinfish (MAN-duh-rin-fish) live among the coral of the Great Barrier Reef.

Just off the east coast, in the Coral Sea, is the Great Barrier Reef. The ocean there is as warm as bathwater. It is so clear, it is easy to see the fish swimming all around. The corals provide food and shelter for many animals, including the green sea turtle and the brightly colored mandarinfish.

The box jellyfish is almost invisible when underwater.

The box jellyfish is the most dangerous jellyfish in the world. Its stinging tentacles **(TEN-tih-kulz)** can be over 10 feet long.

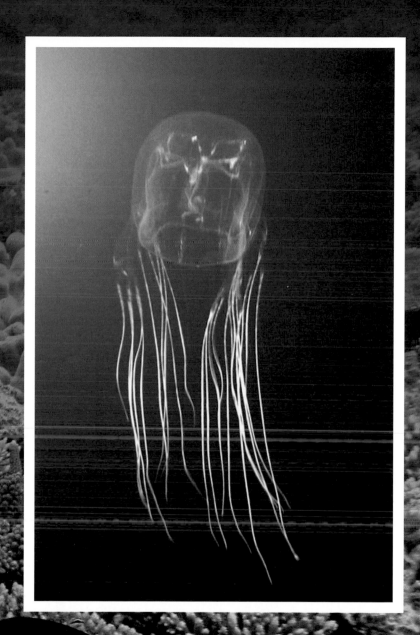

Hammerhead sharks are one of the few fish that can get a tan from the sun.

Just past the reef, hammerhead sharks feast on squid and schools of sardines. Unlike other sharks, these travel in groups. They get their name from the hammer-like shape of their heads.

Great white sharks are so dangerous, they are at the very top of the ocean's food chain. What makes these sharks so dangerous? Their senses! Their noses can smell blood from three miles away.

Baby great white sharks are called pups.

Saltwater crocodiles have the strongest bite of all animals.

Another creature that lurks in the sea is the saltwater crocodile **(KROK-oh-dy-al)**. Its jaws are very powerful, but it cannot chew its prey. It must swallow it whole. The average weight of these crocs is 1,000 pounds. Some can weigh a ton or more.

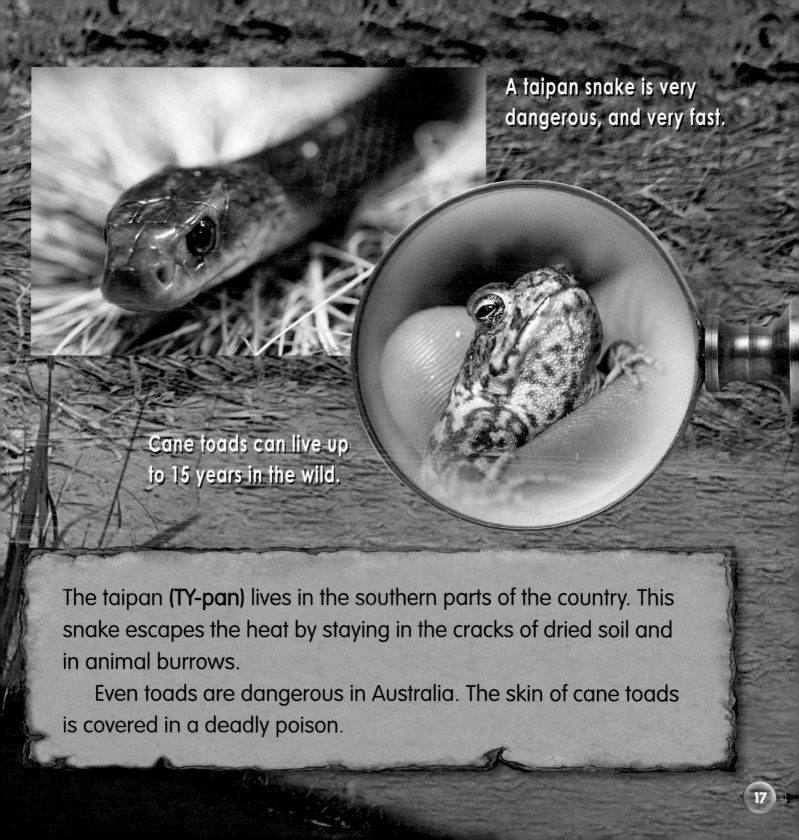

A taipan snake is very dangerous, and very fast.

Cane toads can live up to 15 years in the wild.

The taipan (TY-pan) lives in the southern parts of the country. This snake escapes the heat by staying in the cracks of dried soil and in animal burrows.

Even toads are dangerous in Australia. The skin of cane toads is covered in a deadly poison.

Sydney funnel web spiders mostly stay inside their underground homes. They come out only to hunt.

Australians know to wear long pants tucked into their socks because of some dangerous insects outside. None are more dangerous than the Sydney funnel web spider. Its venom makes it one of the deadliest spiders on the planet.

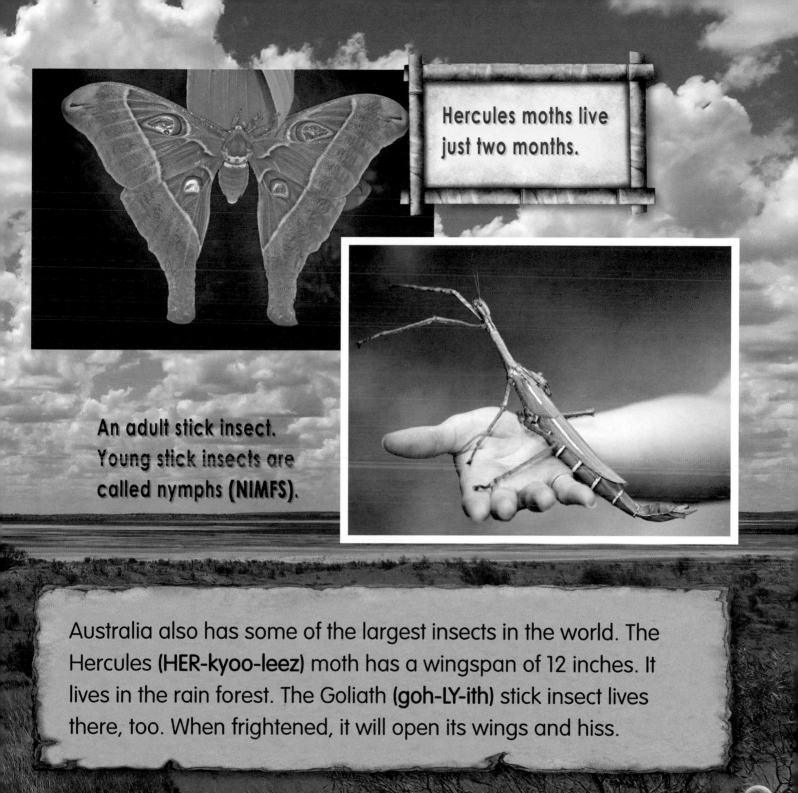

An adult stick insect. Young stick insects are called nymphs (NIMFS).

Australia also has some of the largest insects in the world. The Hercules (HER-kyoo-leez) moth has a wingspan of 12 inches. It lives in the rain forest. The Goliath (goh-LY-ith) stick insect lives there, too. When frightened, it will open its wings and hiss.

Wombats waddle when they walk just like penguins do. And, believe it or not, a wombat's poop is square.

Dingoes are part of the dog family, but they can't bark like dogs. They can only howl. Their favorite food is meat, but they like fruits, grains, and nuts, too.

Whether you are swimming on the Great Barrier Reef or hiking in the Australian bush, this continent has much to offer.

A dingo will bury extra food to save it for later.

FURTHER READING

Books

Eileen, Hirsch Rebecca. *Australia.* New York, NY: Scholastic, 2012.

Friedman, Mel. *Australia and Oceania.* New York, NY: Children's Press, 2009.

Olson, Nathan. *Australia in Colors.* North Mankato, MN: Capstone Press, 2008.

Scillian, Devin. *D is for Down Under: An Australia Alphabet.* Ann Arbor, MI: Sleeping Bear Press. 2010.

Works Consulted

Animal Diversity Web, University of Michigan Museum of Zoology
http://animaldiversity.org

Australian Animals: Perth Zoo
http://perthzoo.wa.gov.au/animals-plants/australia/

Australia's Animals
http://www.australia.com/en-us/facts/australias-animals.html

National Geographic: Australia
http://travel.nationalgeographic.com/travel/countries/australia-guide/

Websites

Activity Village: Australia
http://www.activityvillage.co.uk/australian-animals

Oz for Kids
http://www.ozforkids.com/

PBS Kids/Wild KRATTS: Australian Outback
http://pbskids.org/wildkratts/habitats/australian-outback/

biome (BY-ohm)—A community of animals and plants living together in a specific climate.

eucalyptus (yoo-kuh-LIP-tus)—A genus of mostly Australian evergreen trees that are widely cultivated for their gums, resins, oils, and useful woods.

Great Barrier Reef (grayt BAR-ee-er reef)—The largest coral reef in the world. It is in the Coral Sea off the northeastern coast of Australia.

lunge (luhnj)—A sudden forward movement.

marsupial (mar-SOO-pee-ul)—Any of the mammals with pouches for carrying their babies.

population (pop-yuh-LAY-shun)—All of the animals or people in one area.

savanna (suh-VAN-uh)—A flat grassland in a tropical area.

Tasmanian (taz-MEY-nee-en)—An inhabitant of the island Tasmania, south of Australia.

venom (VEH-num)—Poison produced by an animal.

INDEX

Printing   1   2   3   4   5   6   7   8   9

The Animals of Africa
The Animals of Antarctica
The Animals of Asia
The Animals of Australia
The Animals of Europe
The Animals of North America
The Animals of South America

ABOUT THE AUTHOR: Nicole Orr has been writing for as long as she's known how to hold a pen. She's the author of three other titles by Purple Toad Publishing and has won National Novel Writing Month nine times. Orr lives in Portland, Oregon, and camps under the stars whenever she can. When she isn't writing, she's traveling the world or taking road trips. When she was living in Brisbane, Australia, she had the chance to meet an ibis. It tried to steal her french fries!

Publisher's Cataloging-in-Publication Data
Orr, Nicole K.
   Australia / written by Nicole K. Orr.
      p. cm.
Includes bibliographic references, glossary, and index.
ISBN 9781624692642
1. Animals—Australia—Juvenile literature. I. Series: A continent of creatures.
   QL338 2017
   591.994

eBook ISBN: 9781624692659

Library of Congress Control Number: 2016937184